Study Guide

SEVEN SIMPLE SECRETS
What the BEST Teachers Know and Do

Annette Breaux and Todd Whitaker

D1736654

Nancy Satterfield

EYE ON EDUCATION
6 DEPOT WAY WEST, SUITE 106
LARCHMONT, NY 10538
(914) 833–0551
(914) 833–0761 fax
www.eyeoneducation.com

10 9 8 7 6 5 4 3 2 1

Editorial and production services provided by
Hypertext Book and Journal Services
738 Saltillo St., San Antonio, TX 78207-6953 (210-227-6055)

Table of Contents

Introduction

This study guide has been developed to accompany the *Seven Simple Secrets* book written by Dr. Todd Whitaker and Annette Breaux. *Seven Simple Secrets* focuses on those attributes that have been found to be the keys for being your absolute best as a classroom teacher. This study guide can help you reflect on how the seven secrets can assist you in your daily challenges of teaching and improving student learning.

The study guide is divided into the Seven Secrets and the seven qualities found within each Secret. The book and study guide can be used in a sequential manner or teachers and staff can select the Secret on which they wish to focus.

At the end of each Secret is a summary checklist that you can complete prior to your work with these materials. Following your discussions with these ideas and suggestions, you can complete the checklist to see if there have been improvements to your teaching strategies.

Seven Simple Secrets is not another "program" you have to follow or learn. It is, simply, those proven techniques utilized by the most effective teachers. By embracing these ideas, you will become a more effective teacher. What a wonderful accolade for a teacher to be told by their students "You're the Best Teacher I've Ever Had!" Don't you want to hear that too?

Let's begin the process by discussing the ideas presented in the book and study guide in order to ensure an exciting and rewarding school year.

Secret One:
The Secret of Planning

Part One: How to Have a Great Plan

The very best teachers know that to have a great lesson—you need to plan a great lesson.

How to Have a Great Plan outlines the many reasons that you should take the time to plan a good lesson.

1. What were your thoughts regarding planning as you read this section?

    _____

    _____

    _____

2. How much time do you use each week for lesson planning?

    _____

    _____

    _____

3. What are the key components to good lesson plans?

    _____

    _____

    _____

    _____

    _____

    _____

4. Do you currently have all those components in your lessons?

    _____

    _____

    _____

    _____

5. Take a copy of a recent lesson plan and highlight the key components as identified in question 3. Share your lesson plan with your team or a colleague and discuss the steps you go through when planning your lesson.

_____

_____

_____

_____

_____

_____

_____

6. Identify steps you can take to improve your lesson plan.

_____

_____

_____

_____

_____

_____

7. Create two great lesson plans using the key components identified. Implement the plans. Following the implementation of each plan, reflect on the differences you noticed in your classroom regarding student engagement, student understanding, and classroom management.

_____

_____

_____

_____

_____

Part Two: How to Overplan

The very best teachers, as part of their secret to successful planning, always Overplan.

1. Have you ever had a day when your plans didn't take as long as you had anticipated? Describe what happened.

_____

_____

_____

_____

_____

_____

_____

_____

Share your experience with your team and/or a colleague.

2. Take one lesson and provide two "overplanning" activities. Share this plan with your team and/or a colleague discussing how and why you planned these activities. Also, discuss how these activities can be used in a future lesson if they are not used in the current plan.

_____

_____

_____

_____

_____

_____

_____

_____

Part Three: How to Manage Your Time

Some of the very best teachers plan their lessons in 5-minute segments.

1. The authors illustrate how planning a lesson in 5-minute segments allows for more variety in the activities and more engagement of the students. Take a lesson plan you recently implemented. Describe your time allotments for YOUR lesson.

    _____

    _____

    _____

    _____

    _____

    _____

    Share your experience with your team and/or a colleague.

2. Using 5-minute segments, plan an upcoming lesson. Teach the lesson and reflect on how this approach worked for you and your students.

    _____

    _____

    _____

    _____

    _____

    _____

    Share the results with a colleague and/or your team. Continue to refine your lessons utilizing the 5-minute segments approach.

Part Four: How to be Flexible

The very best teachers know that flexibility is a must in planning.

As the authors stated, "best laid plans" often don't go as planned. This section focuses on how you cope with interruptions during your day.

1. Do you consider yourself flexible when it comes to your daily routines and interruptions in your routines?

    _____

    _____

    _____

2. How can a teacher be less distracted by interruptions? Describe how you would help a new teacher to deal with these situations.

    _____

    _____

    _____

    Share these tips with a colleague and/or your team.

3. What would you suggest to the administration as possible solutions to minimize interruptions in your school?

    _____

    _____

    _____

    _____

    Share your ideas with your team and/or principal.

Part Five: How to Make Objectives Clear

Making objectives clear is vital to helping students learn. Students must have a clear understanding of what they are to learn during a lesson.

1. In your own words describe the difference in lesson activities and lesson objectives.

    _____

    _____

    _____

    _____

    _____

2. Review your lesson plans for the past week. Did you clearly identify your objectives for the lessons?

    _____

    _____

    _____

    _____

    _____

3. Give two examples of effective objectives.

    _____

    _____

    _____

    _____

    _____

4. For an upcoming lesson, make sure that the lesson focuses on the objectives (skills and knowledge you want your students to know) and then support the objectives with various activities. Have a colleague and/or team member review your lesson for clarity and focus.

Notes

_____

_____

_____

_____

_____

_____

_____

_____

_____

_____

_____

_____

_____

_____

_____

_____

_____

_____

_____

_____

_____

_____

_____

_____

_____

_____

_____

_____

_____

Part Six: How to Promote Activity

We know that whoever is doing the "doing" is doing the learning. In your classroom, are the students "doing" the work or are you—the teacher—the person most actively engaged?

The authors recommend planning with questions that foster higher order thinking.

1. Review a recent lesson plan and list several of the questions you asked your students.

_____

_____

_____

_____

_____

_____

_____

_____

_____

_____

_____

Share these questions with a colleague and/or your team and discuss how these questions did or did not promote higher order thinking.

_____

_____

_____

_____

_____

2. Do you have your classroom set up for hands-on learning, cooperative grouping, or student presentations? If not, think of ways you can incorporate at least one of these activities in a lesson plan within the next 2 weeks.

_____

_____

_____

_____

_____

_____

Reflect on how successful these activities were in your classroom.

_____

_____

_____

_____

_____

_____

Share your experience with a colleague and/or team member. If the lesson was successful, plan for future activities incorporating the strategy. If the lesson was not successful, determine what could be done differently to have your students engaged in their learning. Ask a colleague and/or team member for help if needed.

_____

_____

_____

_____

_____

Part Seven: How to Be Proactive

Being proactive means anticipating typical problems and warding them off before they take place.

The authors use the examples of Ms. Reactive and Ms. Proactive to illustrate the concept of being proactive when planning new lessons and activities for your students. Are you more proactive or reactive? Explain.

_____

_____

_____

_____

_____

Discuss with your colleague and/or team members strategies that can be used in classrooms that would be considered proactive. Make a list for all to see and use.

_____

_____

_____

_____

_____

As you plan for an upcoming lesson, think about these strategies and include one or more into your lesson. Reflect on how the strategy enhanced your lesson.

_____

_____

_____

_____

_____

Secret One Summary Checklist

Mark the columns that you feel best represent where you currently are regarding the strategies identified.

STRATEGIES	1	2	3
1. Do you feel that you have great lesson plans?			
2. Are your plans clear with specific objectives?			
3. Do your lessons reflect your student's interests and involvement in their learning?			
4. Do you follow the 60/40 rule?			
5. Do you always overplan your lessons?			
6. Do you manage your time in 5-minute segments?			
7. Are you flexible and able to adapt to changes in your routines?			
8. Are you able to focus on what you *can* control and not on what you can't?			
9. Are your lesson objectives outcome specific?			
10. Are your objectives supported by appropriate activities?			
11. Are you positive in your actions rather than negative in reactions?			

1 = Rarely or never in my classroom;
2 = Sometimes in my classroom;
3 = On a consistent basis in my classroom.

Secret Two:
The Secret of
Classroom Management

Part One:
What an Effective Teacher's Classroom Looks Like

The authors provided lists of what can be observed in more-effective and less-effective classrooms.

1.   Think back to a teacher you had that would be an example of a "less-effective teacher" and describe what occurred in that classroom and its effect on your learning.

_____

_____

_____

_____

_____

_____

Share your reflections with a colleague and/or team members.

2.   Now think about a teacher you had that would be an example of a "more effective teacher" and describe what occurred in that classroom and its effect on your learning.

_____

_____

_____

_____

_____

_____

Share your reflections with a colleague and/or team members.

Think about what you and your colleagues identified as "effective teaching." Does this describe your classroom?

Select two or three traits and incorporate them into your classroom for the next 2 weeks. At the end of that time, describe any positive differences you experienced as a result.

_____

_____

_____

_____

_____

_____

_____

_____

_____

_____

_____

_____

Share these experiences with your colleagues and/or team members.

Notes

_____

_____

_____

_____

_____

_____

Part Two:
The Difference Between Rules and Procedures

A rule *is something that regulates serious student misbehavior. A* procedure *is simply a way that you expect something to be done.*

1. Identify two or three **rules** that you have established in your classroom.

_____

_____

_____

_____

2. Identify two or three **procedures** that you have established in your classroom.

_____

_____

_____

_____

Share these lists with your colleagues and/or team members. Does everyone agree on what is a rule and what is a procedure? Have a discussion regarding the lists if there are any differences of opinion.

3. For each of the rules you listed, identify the consequence if the rule is broken.

_____

_____

_____

_____

_____

4. How often do you have to enforce the rules on a daily basis?

_____

_____

_____

_____

5. How do you teach the procedures you want followed in your classroom?

_____

_____

_____

_____

_____

6. Are you consistent with the implementation of your procedures? Describe what you do to ensure that your procedures are followed.

_____

_____

_____

_____

_____

_____

_____

_____

_____

_____

_____

Part Three: How to Establish Rules and Procedures

The most effective teachers have very few rules.

1. In Part Two you were asked to list your classroom rules. In Part Three the authors have outlined seven steps to establishing and maintaining classroom rules. Are these steps similar to how you established your classroom rules? Describe the similarities and the differences.

    _____

    _____

    _____

    _____

    _____

2. How effectively do you feel you discuss the rules of the classroom with your students, and how do you teach the rules to new students who come into your class throughout the school year?

    _____

    _____

    _____

    _____

    _____

3. Can you improve on how you establish and maintain the rules in your classroom? Describe some steps you could take to improve this part of your classroom management.

    _____

    _____

    _____

    _____

    _____

4. In Part Two you were asked to identify classroom procedures you expect your students to follow. In Part Three the authors describe the process that the most effective teachers use when establishing procedures. Are these steps similar to how you establish your procedures? Describe the similarities and differences.

_____

_____

_____

_____

_____

_____

5. How effective do you think you have been in establishing classroom procedures with your students, and how do you teach them to students who are new to your classroom throughout the year?

_____

_____

_____

_____

_____

_____

6. Can you improve on establishing and maintaining effective classroom procedures for your students? Describe steps you could take to improve this part of your classroom management.

_____

_____

_____

_____

_____

Part Four: What to Do if Your Student's "Don't"

In this section the authors have provided examples of what *not* to do and what *to* do when students don't follow your rules and procedures.

1. As you read this section, reflect on which of the methods for following *rules* best describes your response during a typical day with your students.

    _____

    _____

    _____

    _____

2. Which of the methods for following *procedures* best describes your response during a typical day?

    _____

    _____

    _____

    _____

3. Following rules and procedures is critical to maintaining good classroom management. Discuss with your colleagues/team members what you do when students don't follow your rules and procedures. Create a list of tips and suggestions that have been effective in having students understand and follow rules and procedures. Share this list.

    _____

    _____

    _____

    _____

    _____

    _____

    _____

Part Five: Bell-to-Bell Teaching

The busier students are, the less time they have to misbehave. And the busier they remain, the better their achievement.

1. The authors state that teaching from bell to bell means having *the students actively engaged in meaningful activities.* Describe strategies/activities you use to get your students busy as soon as they get to class.

    _____

    _____

    _____

    _____

    _____

    _____

2. List three activities that have been proven to be effective in engaging students in learning as soon as they are seated. Share your ideas with your colleagues.

    _____

    _____

    _____

3. The authors used the example of letting students have 2 to 3 minutes of nothing to do at the end of the period. Create a list of activities that have been proven to be effective in keeping students engaged until the dismissal bell if the lesson ended a few minutes early. Share this list with your colleagues.

    _____

    _____

    _____

    _____

    _____

Part Six: How to Discipline Proactively

Less-effective teachers run around putting out fires while more effective teachers practice fire prevention.

1. In this section the authors use two scenarios to illustrate the difference in effective responses to students being off-task in the classroom. Discuss the scenarios with your colleagues/team members and discuss the effective teachers' responses.

2. In this section the authors use two scenarios to illustrate the ineffective responses to students being off-task in the classroom. Discuss the scenarios with your colleagues/team members and discuss the ineffective teachers' responses.

_____

_____

_____

_____

_____

_____

_____

3. Reflect on your past week of teaching. Which of the teachers described would you say best describes your discipline approach? If you are more reactive than proactive, what steps can you take to change how you discipline misbehaviors in your classroom? If you are proactive, what can you do to be even more proactive?

_____

_____

_____

_____

_____

_____

_____

Part Seven: How NOT to be a Screamer

It is never appropriate or effective to yell or scream at a student.

1. The authors state that in any school, students and parents can always identify the teachers who are known for raising their voices in an attempt to control their students. The strategy for effective teachers is to respond to misbehavior with a soft-spoken voice. How would your students rate you if asked about your tone of voice?

    _____

    _____

    _____

    _____

    _____

2. Reflect on the statement "the more *out of control* the student—the more *in control* an effective teacher must be." Discuss this statement with your colleagues/team members. Describe scenarios where you have had a student lose control and you used an effective response to diffuse the situation.

    _____

    _____

    _____

    _____

3. Describe a misbehavior situation that you feel could have been handled more effectively. What will you do differently should the same situation occur?

    _____

    _____

    _____

    _____

    _____

Secret Two Summary Checklist

Mark the columns that you feel best represent where you currently are regarding the strategies identified.

STRATEGIES	1	2	3
1. My classroom is organized with "a place for everything and everything in its place."			
2. My lessons are filled with enthusiasm and excitement.			
3. The students do most of the talking and "doing" in my classroom as directed through my questioning and guidance.			
4. I follow routines and procedures in my classroom and my students understand what is expected of them.			
5. I have consistent consequences for broken rules.			
6. I have few, if any, interruptions in my classroom for the purpose of establishing control.			
7. I try to be proactive in all situations.			
8. Anyone could pick up my lessons and know what we are learning in my classroom.			
9. I clearly establish the objectives for the lesson with my students so they know what and why they are learning.			
10. I move around the classroom during my lessons.			
11. My lessons are designed to have the students actively engaged in meaningful activities.			

STRATEGIES	1	2	3
12. I am in control of my classroom and I don't let my students know when I am upset or frustrated.			
13. My lessons are varied to meet the needs of all my students.			
14. I use positive reinforcement in my classroom.			
15. I smile and provide positive comments about my teaching and my students.			
16. I teach from bell to bell.			

1 = Rarely or never in my classroom;
2 = Sometimes in my classroom;
3 = On a consistent basis in my classroom.

Secret Three:
The Secret of Instruction

Part One: How to Teach for Real Life

The authors state that the best teachers define real-life teaching as relating the skills taught to the real lives of the students.

1. Reflect on a recent lesson plan and determine if you made real-life connections in your lesson. Describe the lesson and the real-life link.

    _____

    _____

    _____

    _____

2. Share your teaching experience with a colleague or team members and discuss how often you are able to bring real-life links to student learning.

    _____

    _____

    _____

3. The authors provided two scenarios of different approaches to teaching pronouns. Do you identify with either teacher? If so, which one?

    _____

    _____

    _____

4. The authors state that the best teachers make their lessons exciting and inviting by relating learning to real life. Describe an engaging lesson that you have taught that you feel would meet that criteria.

    _____

    _____

    _____

    _____

Part Two: How to Ensure Active Student Involvement

The authors relate active learning to intentional or meaningful learning.

1. When you look at your classes, do you see students engaged in meaning-ful, intentional learning? Describe a typical class time and the *types of activities* someone would see if they observed your classroom.

    _____

    _____

    _____

    _____

    _____

    _____

    _____

2. Share the types of activities you listed with your colleague and/or team members. Discuss the involvement levels of the students with the various activities.

3. The authors state that all good lessons plan for active student involvement through questioning, real-life links, and active learning. If you were work-ing with a teacher intern, how would you describe your lesson-planning process to him/her? Describe the steps you would use.

    _____

    _____

    _____

    _____

    _____

    _____

    _____

Part Three: How to Ensure Success for All Students

The most effective teachers refuse to believe that there is any such thing as a student not capable of succeeding and achieving.

1. What are your personal thoughts about that statement? Do you agree or disagree? Describe your thoughts.

_____

_____

_____

_____

2. Discuss the statement with your colleagues and/or team members. Does everyone agree with the authors?

_____

_____

_____

_____

3. Describe techniques that you have successfully used to get all your students engaged in your classroom.

_____

_____

_____

_____

_____

4. Share those techniques and ideas with your colleagues and/or team members.

Part Four: How to Teach Enthusiastically

The authors offer two very different teaching styles to illustrate teaching with and without enthusiasm.

1. What were the various teaching strategies that Ms. Enthusiastic utilized in her lesson?

   _____

   _____

   _____

   _____

   _____

2. Would your students rate you as an enthusiastic teacher? If yes, what would they say about you?

   _____

   _____

   _____

   _____

3. If your students would rate you as lacking in enthusiasm, what could you do to change your approach to your teaching?

   _____

   _____

   _____

   _____

4. Discuss with your colleagues activities they have planned that helped foster enthusiasm for learning.

Part Five: How to Align Teaching and Testing

Teachers should test only what they have taught and in the manner that they have taught it.

1. The authors provided several examples of poor testing strategies where the teacher did not test what had been taught. Discuss these examples with a colleague and/or team member as to how this type of testing can be avoided.

2. Describe a recent test that you gave to your students. Was your test aligned with the objectives for learning, and did it test the students as they were taught?

_____

_____

_____

_____

_____

_____

_____

3. What testing methods do you use to determine what your students know? Describe all the testing methods you use in your classroom.

_____

_____

_____

_____

_____

_____

_____

_____

4. Which method do you feel is the best indicator of student learning and why?

_____

_____

_____

_____

_____

_____

_____

_____

_____

_____

5. Share your testing strategies and thoughts with a colleague and/or team member. Use examples to illustrate your testing strategies.

Notes

_____

_____

_____

_____

_____

_____

_____

_____

_____

_____

Part Six: How to Pace Your Lessons Appropriately

Effective instruction ensures that the lesson moves at a quick but appropriate pace for learning.

1. The authors provide a list of eight tips to let you know your lessons are appropriately paced. Look at the list and reflect on your teaching for the past few days. How many of these tips do you think apply to your classroom? Describe which ones could be observed and give examples.

_____

_____

_____

_____

_____

_____

_____

_____

2. The authors also listed seven warning signs for students not engaged in learning. Look at this list and reflect on your teaching for the past few days. How many of these warning signs do you think apply to your classroom? Describe which ones could be observed and give examples.

_____

_____

_____

_____

_____

_____

_____

_____

_____

To improve the pacing of your lessons and the engagement of your students, use the lists to evaluate your teaching. You could also have a colleague observe you or you could videotape yourself to determine how to better pace your lessons for maximum student learning.

3. Select a lesson in the coming week and note your students' behaviors. If you observe some of the warning signs, focus on your future lesson plans to make the activities more engaging. What were the warning signs and what specific activities will you create to avoid a repeat of the behavior?

_____

_____

_____

_____

_____

_____

_____

_____

_____

_____

Notes

_____

_____

_____

_____

_____

_____

_____

_____

_____

Part Seven: How to Teach Anything to Anyone

The authors have discussed the secrets of effective instruction through the first six parts of this chapter. In this chapter they outline the five steps that effective teachers **always** follow when teaching a new skill/concept.

1.   List the five steps.

    1. _____

    2. _____

    3. _____

    4. _____

    5. _____

2.   In reflecting on your teaching methods, do you feel you follow all five steps with each lesson? Describe a recent lesson using the five steps and give examples of what you did to illustrate each step.

_____

_____

_____

_____

_____

_____

_____

_____

_____

3.   Discuss with your colleagues activities or events they have planned that helped foster effective instruction.

Secret Three Summary Checklist

Mark the columns that you feel best represent where you currently are regarding the strategies identified.

STRATEGIES	1	2	3
1. I am able to relate the content I teach to the real lives of my students.			
2. I plan my lessons to include hands-on learning and active student involvement.			
3. I am able to differentiate my instruction to meet the various learning levels of my students.			
4. I am enthusiastic when I am teaching.			
5. I assess my students on the content that I have taught.			
6. My assessments reflect the way I have taught.			
7. I feel that I pace my lessons effectively.			
8. I follow the basic steps for teaching.			
9. I have a clear introduction that relates the content to a student's real life.			
10. As I teach a skill I model it for my students.			
11. After I have taught a skill I practice it with my students.			
12. I reteach the skills if students are struggling with understanding.			

STRATEGIES	1	2	3
13. I let the students try the new skill on their own.			
14. I review with my students by allowing them to demonstrate or tell me what they have learned.			

1 = Rarely or never in my classroom;
2 = Sometimes in my classroom;
3 = On a consistent basis in my classroom.

Secret Four:
The Secret of Attitude

Part One:
How to Be in Control of Your Attitude: It's Up to You!

One of the main things that separates the not-so-good teacher from the good teacher and the good from the great teacher is simply attitude.

1. One point that the authors make is that negative teachers rarely see that quality in themselves. If you were to ask your principal or colleagues about your attitude, what do you think they would say?

_____

_____

_____

_____

_____

2. One way to improve an attitude is to make an effort to limit negative remarks to students and replace those remarks with positive ones. If you were asked to help someone who is too negative—what are some examples or ideas you might share with them?

_____

_____

_____

_____

_____

3. How do YOU deal with a coworker or others who are always negative and complaining?

_____

_____

_____

_____

_____

4. Discuss with your colleagues the negative effects you feel when working with someone who is always negative. What could be done to help that person change their attitude? List possible solutions.

_____

_____

_____

_____

_____

_____

_____

_____

_____

5. Discuss how the negative attitude of a teacher affects the overall behavior and learning of students.

_____

_____

_____

_____

_____

_____

_____

_____

Part Two:
How to Handle Yourself in the Teachers' Lounge

A teachers' lounge should be a place to go and relax for short periods of time during the school day.

1. How would you describe the atmosphere of your teachers' lounge on a typical day?

_____

_____

_____

_____

_____

_____

2. If your teachers' lounge is relaxing and inviting ... Congratulations! However, if you feel it is the common area for griping and complaining, what can you do to change the atmosphere? List several ideas you might have for improving a negative atmosphere.

_____

_____

_____

_____

_____

3. Discuss the teachers' lounge issue with a colleague and/or team members. Does everyone perceive the lounge in the same way? Work together as a team to help create a positive work environment for your faculty workroom or lounge. Implement some of the suggested changes and reevaluate the issue in 1 month to see if improvements have been made.

Part Three:
How to Improve the Attitudes of Your Students

A teacher's attitude carries over to the students and affects their attitudes.

1. The authors gave two examples of how teachers may handle an upset student. Think back to a recent event when a student came in from recess, lunch, or another class and was in a bad mood before they walked into your classroom. How did you handle the situation with the student?

    _____

    _____

    _____

    _____

    _____

2. In looking back at the situation, and given the two examples in the book, do you think you handled it in the best manner? Explain.

    _____

    _____

    _____

    _____

    _____

3. Discuss with your colleagues ways you have successfully redirected a student that came in upset. Share tips and techniques that have been successful for you.

    _____

    _____

    _____

    _____

    _____

4. The authors stated that students are always watching their teachers in order to get their cues for behaviors. A challenge they offered is to ask a student to imitate your behaviors. If you offered this challenge, how do you think your students would act? Describe.

_____

_____

_____

_____

_____

_____

_____

_____

_____

_____

5. If you want to improve how you respond to student behaviors, ask a colleague to observe a class period and give you feedback. Or videotape a lesson and critique your behaviors. You can improve your control when dealing with student misbehaviors but only if you are aware that there is room to improve.

_____

_____

_____

_____

_____

_____

_____

_____

_____

Part Four: How to Portray an Attitude of Responsibility

Effective teachers always assume responsibility for students that are not succeeding in their classroom.

1. The authors use an example of a physician who has many patients dying following surgery and he blames it on their being "unhealthy." Is that a surgeon you would want operating on you? By the same token, many teachers say it is the fault of the students if the students are not learning. Describe your thoughts on this statement.

    _____

    _____

    _____

    _____

    _____

    _____

    _____

2. Share your thoughts with your colleagues and/or team members.

3. Even the most effective teachers with well-planned lessons will have students who are having difficulty learning the content/strategies being taught. What are some techniques you have effectively used to help ALL your students learn. Describe.

    _____

    _____

    _____

    _____

    _____

4. Share some of your techniques/strategies with your colleagues and/or team members. Make a list of teaching tips that others can use.

_____

_____

_____

_____

_____

_____

_____

_____

_____

5. One of the scenarios that the authors provided was regarding students sleeping in class. Reflect on your response in the past when a student started to sleep in your class. Was it in the manner described for an effective teacher? If not, what can you do differently the next time this behavior occurs in your classroom?

_____

_____

_____

_____

_____

_____

_____

_____

6. A second scenario involved the grading of papers by students and then the calling out of grades for all to hear. The authors stated that *"effective teachers grade their students' papers."* If you currently use the described practice, eliminate it from your teaching practices for the betterment of your students' attitudes toward your class and you as a teacher.

Part Five: How to Defuse Negative Coworkers

In earlier parts of the book and study guide you were asked to think about and discuss ways to work with negative colleagues and students.

1. The authors use several scenarios that often occur during the course of the day. Read over them and reflect on what you do when:

    (a) A teacher speaks negatively about a student.

    _____

    _____

    _____

    _____

    (b) A coworker gripes about something that is happening in the school.

    _____

    _____

    _____

    _____

    (c) A coworker gossips about someone at the school—a student, teacher, or the principal.

    _____

    _____

    _____

    _____

    (d) A coworker is reprimanding a student in an unprofessional manner.

    _____

    _____

    _____

    _____

(e) A coworker tries to engage you in a power struggle.

_____

_____

_____

_____

_____

_____

_____

_____

_____

_____

Remember that when dealing with the attitudes and actions of those around you, YOU are in control of *your* response. You can't control others but you can control how you respond to them. Always take the right path and walk away from those who are trying to include you in their negative world.

Notes

_____

_____

_____

_____

_____

_____

_____

_____

Part Six: How to Work Cooperatively With Parents

The very best teachers communicate frequently with the parents of their students.

1. The authors have provided several examples of positive contacts with parents. The first example deals with the beginning of school. Describe a technique you have used to communicate with parents at the beginning of a new school year.

_____

_____

_____

_____

_____

2. Share your strategies with your colleagues/faculty members. Make a list of ideas that all can share.

_____

_____

_____

3. Another parent scenario is the "confrontational parent." Reflect on the strategy provided here. Describe a technique or approach that you have successfully used when dealing with an upset parent.

_____

_____

_____

_____

4. Share your strategy with your colleagues/faculty members. Make a list of ideas that all can share. (These are especially helpful to new teachers.)

Part Seven: How to Have the Best Attitude on the Faculty

The most effective teachers know that to be as effective as they can be, they must portray a positive attitude.

1. The authors ask you to think about the most positive person on the faculty. Was it you? If not, why not? Describe the traits of the most positive person.

    _____

    _____

    _____

2. Ask several positive people how they manage to be so positive. Record their answers.

    _____

    _____

    _____

    _____

    _____

    _____

3. If no one asked you that question, ask yourself why. What steps can you take to be more positive?

    _____

    _____

    _____

    _____

Work to have the best attitude on the faculty. You'll be happier in your job and so will everyone else around you.

Secret Four Summary Checklist

Mark the columns that you feel best represent where you currently are regarding the strategies identified.

STRATEGIES	1	2	3
1. I have a positive attitude toward students, colleagues, and parents.			
2. I try to find something positive in all situations.			
3. I try to find ways to improve situations.			
4. I only bring positive issues to the teachers' lounge.			
5. I try to smooth situations.			
6. I have a personal responsibility for my students' successes.			
7. I won't let myself get caught up with negative comments or negative people.			
8. I initiate positive connections with parents.			
9. I let parents know that their child's success is my primary responsibility as a teacher.			
10. I work to maintain a positive attitude.			

1 = Rarely;
2 = Sometimes;
3 = On a consistent basis.

Secret Five:
The Secret of Professionalism

Part One: How and Why to Dress Professionally

The authors believe that the best teachers act professionally and dress professionally. Thus, their students respect their professionalism.

1. What is the teacher dress expectation for your school?

_____

_____

_____

_____

_____

2. What would you define as "professional dress" for teachers?

_____

_____

_____

_____

_____

3. Do you feel you dress professionally as defined by your definition?

_____

_____

_____

_____

_____

4.. Discuss with your colleagues the importance of dressing for professionalism and respect from the students, parents, and community you serve.

Part Two: How to "Fit In" Without "Falling In"

The authors believe that effective schools have a sense of family and teamwork that results in staff camaraderie and a common purpose.

1. The definition of "falling in" is to get caught up with negative people and situations. How would you counsel someone new to your school so they don't get caught up with staff that are less than positive in their outlook?

    _____

    _____

    _____

    _____

    _____

2. Effective teachers find each other in a school because they have similar outlooks on their jobs, students, and responsibilities. Think of teachers in your school that you feel are "effective teachers." Describe their qualities.

    _____

    _____

    _____

    _____

    _____

3. Discuss with your colleagues and/or team members the importance of creating a positive climate for your students and of working together.

    _____

    _____

    _____

    _____

    _____

Part Three: How to Maintain Control of Your Actions

When you let students know they can get to you—you've given your control to them.

1. The poem "Don't Let Us Know" shares the truth about not letting students know how to get you upset because they will use it to their advantage. Has a student ever gotten to you to the point that you showed how angry you were? Describe the incident and your response.

    _____

    _____

    _____

    _____

2. If this same incident were to occur tomorrow, how would you handle it differently?

    _____

    _____

    _____

    _____

3. The authors list 13 qualities of an effective teacher when dealing with unruly students. If you were to rank them in order of importance, which would be your top three picks? Explain why.

    _____

    _____

    _____

    _____

4. Discuss your choices with your colleagues and/or team members.

5. Which of the traits listed do you feel you could work on to help make you a more effective teacher?

_____

_____

_____

_____

_____

_____

_____

6. Select one and try it for 2 weeks. Reflect on how it made you feel and how your students responded to the change in your response to bad behaviors.

_____

_____

_____

_____

_____

_____

_____

_____

_____

Notes

_____

_____

_____

_____

_____

Part Four:
How and Why to Continue Your Professional Growth

Effective teachers never stop growing professionally.

1. The authors believe that effective teachers continuously look for ways to better their teaching skills and knowledge. Think about a recent workshop/in-service you have attended and tell what you gained from it.

_____

_____

_____

_____

_____

_____

_____

_____

2. Do you work to gain knowledge even when it is not expected or provided by your school/ district? If yes, describe what you have done.

_____

_____

_____

_____

_____

_____

_____

3. Share your learning experiences with your colleagues and discuss how these experiences have assisted you in your teaching.

4. If you have been working through this manual as part of a professional development plan, you are working to learn the components of being a more effective teacher. Reflect on at least one important point that you feel will help you to become a more effective teacher. Describe what you selected and how you will use the information.

_____

_____

_____

_____

_____

_____

_____

_____

_____

_____

Notes

_____

_____

_____

_____

_____

_____

_____

_____

_____

_____

_____

_____

_____

Part Five:
How to Bleed Professionalism Without Cutting Yourself

Don't allow your frustrations to rob you of your dignity and your professionalism, regardless of how tempting it may be.

1. The authors make the point that it is difficult to always maintain a positive outlook but effective teachers work hard to do so. What are some of the challenges you've faced during the past week? Describe them.

_____

_____

_____

_____

2. Do you feel you dealt with the challenges effectively?

_____

_____

_____

_____

3. Is there anything you wish you could have done differently? Explain.

_____

_____

_____

_____

4. Discuss the topic of professionalism with your colleagues and what it means to you.

Part Six: How to *Do* Your Best—Not Be the Best

The true prize in teaching comes from touching a student's life.

1. The authors use comments from several teachers regarding keeping a positive attitude, growing professionally, and maintaining high levels of enthusiasm. Read over these comments and select one to which you can relate. Write your choice.

    _____

    _____

    _____

2. Why did you select this comment/quote? Explain your connection to the quote.

    _____

    _____

    _____

3. Discuss your quote with your colleagues/team members.

4. If you could choose one area to improve on in your teaching, what would it be?

    _____

    _____

    _____

5. Focus on that area for the next 2 weeks, and then come back and reflect on the changes that have occurred as a result of your efforts.

    _____

    _____

    _____

Part Seven:
How to Make Decisions That Benefit Children

Teachers in more effective schools make all decisions based on what is best for students.

1. The authors give examples of two very different schools. In which school would you prefer to teach?

    _____

    _____

2. Which of the two schools best matches the one in which you teach? Explain your thoughts.

    _____

    _____

    _____

    _____

3. What steps can you, other teachers, and the principal take to make your school better?

    _____

    _____

    _____

    _____

4. Discuss your thoughts with your colleagues and determine steps that you and others can take to work toward a more positive learning environment.

    _____

    _____

    _____

5. The authors state that all decisions should be based on what is best for students. Are the plans you made based on what is best for the students? Explain.

_____

_____

_____

_____

_____

_____

_____

Notes

_____

_____

_____

_____

_____

_____

_____

_____

_____

_____

_____

_____

_____

_____

_____

_____

_____

Secret Five Summary Checklist

Mark the columns that you feel best represent where you currently are regarding the strategies identified.

STRATEGIES	1	2	3
1. I conduct myself as a professional.			
2. I consider the way I dress to be professional.			
3. I am comfortable with my skills and knowledge.			
4. I find others who are positive and easy to work with.			
5. I maintain control in all situations in my classroom.			
6. I don't take students' misbehavior personally.			
7. I maintain a calm voice in all situations.			
8. I always attack a problem but never attack a person.			
9. I participate in professional development activities to improve my teaching.			
10. I work to continue to improve myself as a teacher.			
11. I do my best every day.			
12. I keep my students as my main focus.			

1 = Rarely or never in my classroom;
2 = Sometimes in my classroom;
3 = On a consistent basis in my classroom.

Secret Six:
The Secret of Effective Discipline

Part One: How to Hide Your Buttons From Your Students

Letting students know what they can do to upset you gives away your control.

1. The authors used the example of pressing a button on an elevator to illustrate what students try to do to teachers on a daily basis. Do you have a button that can be pushed by students? What is your button?

    _____

    _____

    _____

    _____

2. The authors provide three questions for you to consider. Ask yourself these questions and carefully consider your answers.

    (a) Do students know when they get to me?

        _____

        _____

        _____

    (b) Can they tell that I am aggravated?

        _____

        _____

        _____

    (c) What do I look like when I get aggravated, upset, or frustrated with my students?

        _____

        _____

        _____

3. The authors recommend several suggestions for not letting students know they are getting to you. Read these again and think about your "buttons." Are there other methods that have worked for you when you were trying to "keep your cool" with a student or groups of students? List other techniques you have used.

_____

_____

_____

_____

_____

_____

4. Discuss with your colleagues and/or team members ways to avoid letting students push your buttons. Make a list of suggestions for all to see.

_____

_____

_____

_____

_____

_____

_____

Notes

_____

_____

_____

_____

_____

_____

Part Two: How to Be Consistent With Discipline

One of the best-kept secrets of the very best teachers is that they have very few discipline problems.

1.   The authors state that effective teachers should have a discipline plan and should use it consistently. What is the discipline plan for your classroom?

_____

_____

_____

_____

_____

_____

2.   Does your school have a schoolwide discipline plan that is known to all students, parents, and staff?

_____

_____

_____

_____

_____

3.   Is your discipline plan and/or the school plan consistently enforced?

_____

_____

_____

_____

_____

4. What are your rules and consequences when they are broken?

_____

_____

_____

_____

_____

_____

_____

_____

5. Do your students help with the development of class rules? If not, have you considered allowing them to help set the rules and the consequences? This will help with the enforcement of the rules as the students know up front what will happen if they choose to break a rule. Discuss this with your colleagues and share how you work with your students on the rules. Or, if you don't let them help write the rules, find out if any of your colleagues do and how it works.

_____

_____

_____

_____

_____

_____

_____

_____

_____

_____

_____

Part Three: How to Relieve Stress With Psychology

The very best teachers are the ones who seem the least stressed and have the fewest discipline problems.

1. The authors provide two examples where teachers use positive techniques to deal with students who are not on task. Have you ever used a similar technique? Describe what you have done.

    _____

    _____

    _____

    _____

    _____

    _____

    _____

2. The authors listed several phrases that effective teachers use when working with students. Can you add other examples of complimentary statements?

    _____

    _____

    _____

    _____

    _____

    _____

    _____

3. Share your list with your colleagues and compile a master list for all to share. Use these phrases with students whenever possible and see the results.

Part Four: How to Become Better, Not Bitter

The very best teachers always choose the better, as opposed to the bitter, path.

1. Unfortunately, bitter teachers exist in many schools today. The seven statements that the authors included at the beginning of this section are far too common. As stated in an earlier chapter, a teacher's attitude influences a student's attitude. As you look around your school, hopefully you don't see any bitter teachers. But, if you do, how do you deal with their negative attitudes?

_____

_____

_____

_____

_____

_____

_____

2. If you have an intern teachers or work with a beginning teacher, how would you counsel them to help them avoid becoming a bitter teacher?

_____

_____

_____

_____

_____

3. The authors provide five statements that are attributed to being a better, more effective teacher. Discuss these statements with your colleagues and/ or team members and reflect on them as they apply to you during your daily interactions with your students.

Part Five:
How to Give Students What They Want and Need

If you want to know what students want and need—ask them!

1. The authors provided a list of what students have said they wanted from teachers. Ask your students what they want from teachers and record their statements.

_____

_____

_____

_____

_____

_____

_____

_____

_____

_____

_____

_____

_____

_____

_____

_____

2. An example provided in the book shows where a teacher took the students' statements and created a "Teacher's Creed" to be posted in the classroom. Take your students' statements and make them into a poster for your classroom, not only for you to follow but to have your students follow as well.

Part Six: How to Be Self-Disciplined

If you can't control yourself, you'll never control a group of students.

1. The authors illustrate two very different reactions to a student's misbehavior. On a typical day, which reaction can you relate to the most? Explain.

_____

_____

_____

_____

_____

2. Ms. Rattleless didn't get into a power struggle with Amy in front of the class. How hard is that to do in your classroom? Explain.

_____

_____

_____

_____

_____

_____

3. Why was Ms. Fuse Box's approach unsuccessful?

_____

_____

_____

_____

_____

_____

4. What were the key strategies Ms. Rattleless used in dealing with Amy's outburst?

_____

_____

_____

_____

_____

_____

_____

_____

_____

Notes

_____

_____

_____

_____

_____

_____

_____

_____

_____

_____

_____

_____

_____

_____

Part Seven: How to Find the Good in Every Child

Children who feel good about themselves are much less likely to misbehave than ones who do not.

1. The authors discuss how teachers are trained to look for problems in students: reading deficiencies, behavior problems, special education issues, and so forth. But, on the flip side, teachers are not trained to look for the good in children. As you look around your class, can you identify the "good" qualities in your students? Describe some of the special qualities that you have recognized in your students.

     _____

     _____

     _____

     _____

     _____

     _____

     _____

     _____

2. One example sited in the book was from a teacher who used an Interest Inventory to get to know her students better. What are other ways teachers can get to know their students and let their student know about them?

     _____

     _____

     _____

     _____

     _____

     _____

     _____

Discuss and share the ideas you have listed with your colleagues and/or team members.

3.   Have you ever had a child who might not have been the best student in terms of class work but had another incredible talent? Describe that student and tell what you did to help encourage his/her talent?

_____

_____

_____

_____

_____

_____

_____

_____

_____

_____

_____

_____

Taking the time to find the best in your students allows you to focus on the positive aspects of teaching.

Notes

_____

_____

_____

_____

Secret Six Summary Checklist

Mark the columns that you feel best represent where you currently are regarding the strategies identified.

STRATEGIES	1	2	3
1. I maintain control in my classroom at all times.			
2. I appear calm in all situations.			
3. I have a specific discipline plan that I follow.			
4. I enforce my discipline plan consistently.			
5. I never argue with my students.			
6. I have clear procedures for students in my classroom.			
7. I use psychology to redirect my students' past/possible discipline problems.			
8. I ask my students what they want, need, and expect in my classroom.			
9. I use a Teacher's Creed in my classroom.			
10. I use all situations that occur in my classroom and school to help me grow as a teacher.			
11. I always focus on being a better teacher.			

1 = Rarely or never in my classroom;
2 = Sometimes in my classroom;
3 = On a consistent basis in my classroom.

Secret Seven:
The Secret of
Motivation and Inspiration

Part One:
How to Make Your Excitement Their Excitement

We remember two groups of teachers: the really good ones and the really bad ones!

1. Reflect on the best teacher you ever had. Describe what that teacher did to earn that recognition from you.

_____

_____

_____

_____

_____

_____

2. Now describe the worst teacher you ever had.

_____

_____

_____

_____

_____

_____

3. Is your classroom "Sunny and Bright" or "Cloudy and Dreary"?

_____

_____

_____

_____

_____

4. Does your classroom have the same characteristics that you described in question 1? If yes, good. If no, why not?

_____

_____

_____

_____

_____

_____

_____

_____

5. Effective teachers don't bring their personal problems into their classrooms. They just act as if everything is okay—even when it might not be. If you were counseling a beginning teacher, what would you tell them regarding their attitude with their students and colleagues?

_____

_____

_____

_____

_____

_____

_____

_____

_____

_____

_____

_____

Part Two:
How to Make Every Student
Feel Like Your Favorite Student

All students want and deserve to feel just as valued as every other student in the classroom.

1. The authors provide comments from an effective teacher discussing why and how she tries to make each student feel special. If you were asked the same question, what would your comments be?

_____

_____

_____

_____

_____

_____

_____

_____

2. Effective teachers make genuinely positive comments such as welcoming students back to the classroom and praising those who are behaving as expected. Provide an example of how you incorporate positive comments during your daily student interactions.

_____

_____

_____

_____

_____

_____

_____

_____

3. The authors give examples of anonymous praise and anonymous fussing. Do either of these examples make you reflect on how you greet students coming into your classroom on a typical day? Which would you say better describes you and your interaction with your students?

_____

_____

_____

_____

_____

_____

_____

_____

4. For the next 3 days use the approach of anonymous praise and see how your students respond. Reflect on the students' responses and how anonymous praise worked.

_____

_____

_____

_____

_____

_____

_____

_____

5. Discuss with your colleagues and/or team members how you try to make all students feel as though they are your favorite students. Share ideas and techniques with each other as you work to build positive relationships with your students.

Part Three:
How to Show Personal Interest in Every Student

One of the best ways to motivate and inspire students is to show personal interest in them.

1. The authors used a story about a teacher who didn't bother to inquire about what had happened to a student with a broken leg. The teacher obviously didn't want to know about that student and felt that the student was unmotivated. Do you have any students about whom you know very little?

_____

_____

_____

2. What would you suggest to first-year teachers as a method of getting acquainted with their students and helping their students to know them better as people and not just as their teachers?

_____

_____

_____

_____

_____

_____

_____

3. Knowing about your students can be valuable or detrimental depending on how you use the information. Discuss with your colleagues the ways understanding your students can be of help to you and them. Also discuss why it is important to avoid using information about a student in a negative manner.

Part Four: How to Maximize the Power of Praise

The most effective teachers agree that praise is one of the most powerful tools we can use to positively impact students.

1. The authors used the word SUCCESS to illustrate the components of praise and how it should be incorporated into your daily habits and routines. The letter S stands for Specific and the authors gave examples of how praise must be specific. Think of times you have praised your students in the past week. Was it specific? Explain.

    _____

    _____

    _____

    _____

    _____

2. How did the students respond to the praise?

    _____

    _____

    _____

    _____

    _____

3. The letter U stands for Unconditional. Praise should be given with no thought of anything in return. Give an example of unconditional praise that you have given and how it was received by your students.

    _____

    _____

    _____

    _____

    _____

4. The letter C stands for Credible. Praise should be true and genuine. Students can tell if praise is not genuine. Reflect on the times you have praised students in the last week. Was it true and genuine praise for their efforts? Explain.

_____

_____

_____

_____

_____

_____

5. The letter C also stands for Consistent. A teacher can praise students while they are making the efforts toward the finished product. Tell how you do this with your students.

_____

_____

_____

_____

_____

_____

6. The letter E stands for Enthusiastic. Do you let your students know that you are proud of their efforts and say it with enthusiasm? Again, think of your praise in the past week and reflect on the level of enthusiasm you put into the praise.

_____

_____

_____

_____

_____

7. The letter S stands for Stand Alone. Are you able to give praise as a "stand alone" and not link it to other behaviors of the student? Give an example of "stand alone" praise in your classroom.

_____

_____

_____

_____

_____

_____

8. The letter S stands for Suitable. Is the praise you are giving to students in line with their abilities and expectations? Think about the praise you recently gave a student and determine if it was suitable for the student.

_____

_____

_____

_____

_____

_____

9. Discuss the use of the SUCCESS model with your colleagues. Do all staff use praise in effective and suitable ways? Discuss ways everyone can incorporate the use of praise in their classrooms to motivate students in their learning.

_____

_____

_____

_____

_____

_____

Part Five: How to Use Rewards Appropriately

The real secret to rewards in the classroom is not **if** you use them but if you use them *effectively.*

1. The authors use an example of a middle school that tried a program they hoped would improve student behavior. The program worked when implemented in a positive manner and failed when used as a threat. Has your school attempted a schoolwide behavior program? Explain.

   _____

   _____

   _____

   _____

   _____

2. Would you say the program is working? Is yes, site examples. If no, site the reasons.

   _____

   _____

   _____

   _____

   _____

3. When schoolwide programs fail, is it the fault of the program or those implementing it?

   _____

   _____

   _____

   _____

   _____

4. Do you have a reward system in your classroom and/or school? Describe your rewards and tell what students must do to receive them.

_____

_____

_____

_____

_____

5. Discuss with your colleagues and/or team members the reward systems they use.

_____

_____

_____

_____

_____

6. What would you tell a beginning teacher about rewards for students?

_____

_____

_____

_____

_____

7. What's the best recognition/reward that you can receive as a teacher, either from your principal, colleagues, students, or parents?

_____

_____

_____

_____

_____

Part Six: How to Motivate Unmotivated Students

Effective teachers find ways to reach all students and spark their interest in learning.

1. The authors provided statements from effective teachers and less-than-effective teachers regarding student motivation. What did you feel when you read the different statements.

_____

_____

_____

_____

_____

2. What types of statements do you make regarding student motivation?

_____

_____

_____

_____

_____

3. What are some motivational strategies that you have used to get your students interested in their learning?

_____

_____

_____

_____

_____

_____

_____

4. Discuss with your colleagues strategies they have used to motivate their students. Make a list of ideas to share with everyone.

_____

_____

_____

_____

_____

_____

_____

5. Ask your students what motivates them to learn. Make a list of their suggestions.

_____

_____

_____

_____

_____

_____

_____

6. Make a list of student suggestions and share them with your colleagues.

_____

_____

_____

_____

_____

Part Seven: How to Maximize the Power of YOU

As teachers, how you feel about yourself helps to determine how you treat your students.

1.　As we come to the end of this study guide regarding the 7 Simple Secrets, what impact have the reflections and discussions had on you and your teaching?

_____

_____

_____

_____

_____

2.　This section deals with YOU and how you can stay positive as you teach the students who have been entrusted to your care. Look at the list of eight tips other effective teachers use to stay positive. Do you use any of these tips?

_____

_____

_____

_____

_____

3.　What other tips or strategies do you use to stay focused and positive in your classroom?

_____

_____

_____

_____

_____

4. Discuss with your colleagues and/or team members things they do to remain positive. Make a list of all the ideas.

_____

_____

_____

_____

_____

_____

_____

_____

_____

_____

_____

_____

_____

_____

_____

_____

_____

The choice to be an effective teacher is yours. You can choose to be positive, inspiring, motivating, challenging, and influential for all your students. The tips, ideas, and suggestions found within the book and study guide will provide you with a strong foundation on which to build your blueprints for success in your classrooms. Take the time to discuss, reflect, try new ways, and find out what works best for you and your students.

Remember, teachers, that your influence is powerful. Be it positive or negative, it is lasting. You will live in the hearts of your students long after you are gone from this earth. Your influence is eternal.

Secret Seven Summary Checklist

Mark the columns that you feel best represent where you currently are regarding the strategies identified.

STRATEGIES	1	2	3
1. I am positive with my students.			
2. I am excited and motivated in my classroom.			
3. I find the good points in all my students.			
4. I try to make all students feel like they are my favorite.			
5. I provide specific praise when earned.			
6. I provide unconditional praise when earned.			
7. I provide genuine praise when earned.			
8. I provide praise on a consistent basis to promote positive behaviors.			
9. I provide praise in an enthusiastic manner.			
10. I don't compromise praise by including a negative statement.			
11. I ensure that my praise is suitable for the situation and for the student.			
12. I work hard to motivate my students.			

STRATEGIES	1	2	3
13. I try to make every student feel special in my classroom.			
14. I try to make every student experience success in my classroom.			

1 = Rarely or never in my classroom;
2 = Sometimes in my classroom;
3 = On a consistent basis in my classroom.

If you would like information about inviting Annette Breaux to speak to your group, please contact her at abreaux@educationspeakersgroup.com

If you would like information about inviting Todd Whitaker to speak to your group, please contact him at t-whitaker@indstate.edu or www.toddwhitaker.com or (812) 237-2904.

If you enjoyed this book, we recommend:

What Great Teachers Do *Differently*

14 Things That Matter Most

Todd Whitaker

"This book is easy to read and provides essential information.
I've ordered copies for every one of my teachers."

—*Ann Ferell, Principal*
Autrey Mill Middle School, GA

What if all your teachers could be just like the best teachers?

This book focuses on the specific things that great teachers do that others do not. It describes the beliefs, behaviors, attitudes, and interactions that form the fabric of life in our best classrooms and schools.

What Great Teachers Do Differently answers these essential questions—

♦ Is it high expectations for students that matter?

♦ How do great teachers respond when students misbehave?

♦ Do great teachers filter differently than their peers?

♦ How do the best teachers approach standardized testing?

♦ How can your teachers gain the same advantages?

2004, 144 pp. paperback 669-1 $29.95 plus shipping and handling

Also available—

Study Guide: What Great Teachers Do *Differently*: 14 Things that Matter Most

Beth Whitaker and Todd Whitaker

2006, 96 pp. paperback 7024-X $16.95 plus shipping and handling

Save $$$ on multiple copy orders!
To order and for details, contact Eye On Education at
888-299-5350 or www.eyeoneducation.com

101 "ANSWERS" FOR NEW TEACHERS AND THEIR MENTORS

Effective Teaching Tips for Daily Classroom Use

Annette L. Breaux

"There is no one I can recommend
more highly than Annette Breaux."

—Harry K. Wong, Author
THE FIRST DAYS OF SCHOOL

This best selling book helps new and experienced teachers develop essential teaching skills which include classroom management, skillful planning, and motivating students. This book:

♦ generates instant impact on teaching and learning;

♦ supports and sustains master classroom teachers who need help mastering their roles as mentors;

♦ stimulates and organizes interactive sessions between new teachers and their mentors;

♦ provides a collection of "thought provokers" and teaching tips for new teachers; and

♦ offers common sense strategies for any teacher seeking to be more effective.

2003, 180 pp. paperback 648-9 $29.95 plus shipping and handling

Save $$$ on multiple copy orders!
To order and for details, contact Eye On Education at
888-299-5350 or www.eyeoneducation.com

Books and Media From Annette Breaux & Todd Whitaker

From Annette Breaux

- *7 Simple Secrets.* 7021-5. $29.95 plus shipping and handling
- *Study Guide, 7 Simple Secrets.* 7066-2. $16.95 plus s&h
- *101 "Answers" for New Teachers and Their Mentors.* 648-9. $29.95 plus s&h
- *The Poetry of Annette Breaux.* 692-6. $19.95 plus s&h
- *Real Teachers, Real Challenges, Real Solutions.* 664-0. $24.95 plus s&h
- *10 Days to Maximum Teaching Success.* 690-X. $299.95 plus s&h
- Additional PALS. 688-8. $8.95 plus s&h. (Contact us for other special prices.)

From Todd Whitaker

- *7 Simple Secrets.* 7021-5. $29.95 plus s&h
- *Study Guide, 7 Simple Secrets.* 7066-2. $16.95 plus s&h
- *Dealing With Difficult Parents.* 609-8. $29.95 plus s&h
- *Dealing With Difficult Teachers.* 645-4. $29.95 plus s&h
- *Feeling Great.* 638-1. $24.95 plus s&h
- *Great Quotes for Great Educators.* 682-9. $29.95 plus s&h
- *Motivating and Inspiring Teachers: Staff Morale.* 099-4. $34.95 plus s&h
- *Six Types of Teachers.* 685-3. $29.95 plus s&h
- *Teaching Matters: Motivating and Inspiring Yourself.* 635-7. $24.95 plus s&h
- *What Great Teachers Do* **Differently.** 669-1. $29.95 plus s&h
- *Study Guide, What Great Teachers Do* **Differently.** 7024-X. $16.95 plus s&h
- *DVD, What Great Teachers Do* **Differently.** 7053-3. $499.00 plus s&h
- *DVD, Great Teachers Facilitator's Guide.* 7051-7. $16.95 plus s&h
- *What Great Principals Do* **Differently.** 647-0. $29.95 plus s&h
- *Study Guide, What Great Principals Do* **Differently.** 7035-5. $16.95 plus s&h
- *DVD, What Great Principals Do* **Differently.** 7052-5. $499.00 plus s&h
- *DVD, Great Principals Facilitator's Guide.* 7050-9. $16.95 plus s&h

Save $$$ on multiple copy orders!
To order and for details, contact Eye On Education at
888-299-5350 or www.eyeoneducation.com